I am an Addict, My name is Dennis

Dennis Cockerham

pencil

ISBN 978-93-5458-756-6

Published in India 2021 by Pencil

A brand of
One Point Six Technologies Pvt. Ltd.
123, Building J2, Shram Seva Premises,
Wadala Truck Terminal, Wadala (E)
Mumbai 400037, Maharashtra, INDIA
E connect@thepencilapp.com
W www.thepencilapp.com

Author biography

A note to you

A Letter To Me

Dennis Cockerham

Born

Son of Rory and Sue

West Point, Nebraska

March 28, 1972

You don't remember this

You used to live with your parents

There was a family

There was a mom

There was a dad

Brother and sisters

Two boys

Two girls

Stacey

Dennis

Christine

Chad

Living in a house

All together

Normal

Parents divorced 1976

That is how Stacey and yourself

Stacey

Older than you by one year

Ended up living with grandma and grandpa

Dad

Originally from Iowa

Went Back

Mom wanted a fresh start

Four kids was too much

She moved

Norfolk, Nebraska

She took Christine and Chad with her

Stacey and you

Signed over

Guardianship to James and Myrtle Webb

Mom's

Mom and dad

Our grandparents

As unbelievable as this is going to sound right now

It won't

You will come to believe great things

Through your experiences in this life

I write to me

Of the past

A way of introduction

To the reader of the present

To introduce us to the world

I

You

Us

We

Almost 50 years old as I write this

Such a distance

From where you are now

Some of this may seem hard to follow

Even now the emotions resonate

Distract me

Yet I promise you

I know your tastes

Pulled to the adventure as you are

Like the themes you make up as you play

Hot wheel cars in the basement

Riding the edge of the law

Like The Dukes Of Hazzard

Doing bad to do good

So many years later

I understand

I understand this contradiction

Repeat

Recreate the same theme

Over and over

In new and inventive ways

In the safety of your imagination

In the basement

Alone

Where nobody comes

I don't want to take these times from you

These moments of peace

This way you play out the confusion

Now your life

Replicating it in your favor

Finally the hero

Loved by all

Yet

There is a reason

Why I have chosen now to reach out to you

It has been brought to your attention

Things at home

Not as they should be

You did not break the swing set

You did not throw the first high heel shoe

You are not a liar

You are not worthless

You do not deserve what comes next

Right does not

Have the same outcome as wrong

Bad and good

Are not the same thing

A plan has been put into place

A way out

No more pain

You are thinking

You are about to take it

I am not going to tell you not to

I know

I still feel the aches

You are hiding under those clothes

I still get lost in the confusion

The tears you shed

The sense of failure

After another try

A try to do right

To do good

To receive praise

To get her attention

To have her love you too

Relief

It is necessary

I do

However

Want to give you an understanding

The weight of this decision

In the basement

With the hot wheels

You always get away

Stealing from the rich

Giving to the poor

Police chasing you

You do not get beaten

You do not get caught

You get away

No punishment

This fantasy

That you created

This hope that you need to be true

This possibility

It is not

I write this letter to you

Just released

The United States Federal Bureau Of Prisons

Sentenced May 12, 2018

55 months

Possession Of A Firearm

This charge itself

Does nothing to explain the process

This is your 7th incarceration

Since turning 18 years old

Prison3 times in Iowa

2 times in South Dakota

This is your second Federal number

Prior to these events

You spent close to 8 years

State Of Nebraska Juvenile System

Starting shortly after reading this letter

In just hours from now

You run away

The decision

Based on fear

On the confusion

On the injustice

It creates the pattern for the rest of your life

And you don't even realize it

Until today

It is not all bad

We are not alone

I write this letter to you now

Too introduce us to the world

We are part of something

Something greater than ourselves

Able to share our journey

Our life

All it entails

With many

Those themes

We imagined in the basement

Those stories we put together

To make our world make sense

It is these very things

They inspire

Motivate

Give the ability to communicate

To ourself

To others

To express the way we think

The way we feel

The way we relate

Let our hope be

That each reader understand

We are not proposing

That we have the answer

But instead

Through our examples

Our path toward a solution

This running away

From the feelings

From the problems

It need not be taken

IT DOES NOT WORK

And to you

Me

The impact

The abuse

The addiction

The contradiction

The realization

It is precisely these things that brings us together today

Finally complete

No longer torn

With strength and courage

Resilience to Reform

Love You,

Me.

CONTENTS

My First Plug

I don't know

If most people

Can look back on their life

See it with clarity

Exactly how

Exactly when

That defining moment happened...

I can

It was 1985

I had been just recently released

A jjuvenile detention center

Located in Lincoln, Nebraska

This time

I was released

To the custody of my mother

Norfolk, Nebraska

There was always

Some unsettled type

Of air in this arrangement

My mother harbored

Lived with the idea

That I blamed her

Leaving me to be raised

By my grandparents

Her mom and dad

I was 13 years old

Not capable of deciphering

Or understanding

This type of psychological dysfunction

That did not stop the brainstorm

The thunder and lighting

Her self-guilt

This always made our relationship

Now our living conditions

Uncomfortable

So

I did what I knew how to do

The lesson

I had been taught

I left

I ran away

I hit the streets

Adept at knowing where to look

Who to talk to

What to say

To become a part of

Any street crowd

After just a couple days

I find him

Just a few houses down the street

From where my mother lived

His name was Gill

And he became

What I would call today

As my first plug

My hook up

My main man

Nope

Gill did not pedal heroin

Meth

Or weed

For that matter

He was

Too broken

Just like me

But he was creative

Gill introduced me

To huffing gasoline

He had me sneak

Over to my mother's house

Grab her gas can

Out of the shed

The one that she kept

For her lawn mower

A tall

Metal can

Adjustable nozzle

As well as the yellow air breather cap

On the very top

When you would go to pour the gas

You would flip it open

The gas would flow more freely

Mine was set up a little different

A rag wrapped around the nozzle

And I ripped that little yellow cap clean off

I would inhale the fumes

My fingers covering the breather hole

As the can indented

When finally I could get no more air

I would release my finger

WHOOSH

The very 1st gasoline bong

Choke included

A couple of rips off that baby

All other feelings faded away

The world became a better place

I did not go anywhere without my gas can

Main street

The park

And in the stores

As you can imagine

This did not go unnoticed

My mother was forced to take some sort of action

Knowing

Direct communication with me

That would probably not be successfull

She found Gill

As the story goes

Gill found me

He sat me down

He told me that I needed to listen to him

Now you must understand

In my world

Gill was my guy

So I listened

He told me that I needed to stop huffing gas

He explained

I could possibly die

There was even a chance

I could get lead poisoning

I heard what Gil told me

I took this information very seriously

As soon as I left Gill

I went to my mother's house

I found 15 cents of spare change

I took that gas can up the street

To the convenience store

I rinsed it out with a nickel

Then...

Then I filled it up with ten cents of UNLEADED

That's right

I had thought it through

Dying was one thing

But walking around with lead poison

That was completely different !.

AUTHORS NOTE : I eventually switched back to thre regular. Even then, I knew...

no addict likes the cut stuff !

Karate Kid

In the midst of addiction
We wear many masks

I would expand
Include
Personas and costumes

Addiction defined
Not just
The use of drugs

Obsessive thinking
Compulsive behavior
Manifestations

Of escapism

I started

Creating

Wearing

Perfecting

My masks

At an early age

A teenager

Alone

Confused

On the streets

Fending for myself

Child abuse

Taken out of the home

Placed in the care of

The State Of Nebraska

Care

I really didn't care for

So I set out

Destined to live

The distortion ingrained in me

Fear

I had no idea

How to survive

To fight

What fighting was

That there was any defense

Other than

To run away

I had been beaten

It was one-sided

It seemed like all the time

I was

No good

Would amount to nothing

This was

What the world did

To the likes of me

But

The mid 80s

All that changed

A punk

A thief

A runaway

I sneaked into a theater

Downtown

Lincoln, Nebraska

The ever-winding path

That led me

Set that day

That day

I watched

In amazement

On the big screen

A skinny little nerd

Scared

Beat up

All the time

Ran into this old

Japanese guy

That taught him karate

After
I lived at that movie
And all theaters
Showing martial art shows

I practiced every single
Wax on, wax off
Sand the floor
And
Paint the fence

I imagined
Always looking eye
And
Don't forget to breathe
Very important

I started telling

All the street kids

That I knew karate

Proceeding

With the proof

My newly mimicked moves

Not only

Did people

Not try to hurt me

They were afraid

I might be able to hurt them

Empowered

Inspired

Highly motivated

I put forth

Any effort necessary

To continue

To build

My very first self-taught

Form of coping

In luck

It was the era

Two more Karate Kid sequels

Bloodsport

Kickboxer

Dojos

Popping up

All over town

To get started

Free lessons

I hit them all

My story grew
With each viewing
Each visit
To a new school

I tore tendons
In my legs
To do the splits
Like Van Damme

Everybody
Thought I was tough

If they called my bluff
Those stretches

Came in handy

I would run

Fast as hell

As I grew

So did the tales

No longer contained

To my fighting abilities

Reaching

Into every area

Of my life

Whomever

Whatever

I needed to be

To accomplish

Whichever thing

I deemed important

At each time

That is

What I was

One identity

To the next

So many stories

One would think

I would lose track

Forget

What I had already said

Not I

Effortlessly

It came to me

Having learned the secret

Knowing

Enough

Telling enough truth

Giving each

A foundation

Able to bend

To flow

One to another

Of course

It was not long

The world

Had seen

Karate Kid

My gig

Seemed to be up

But

Something

Had happened to me

True or not

A valuable lesson

Discovered

A new way

For me

To deal

With fear

All I had to do

Was

Lie!

AUTHORS NOTE : At the age of 37, I entered into an amateur caged mixed martial arts competition in Iowa,

And I won a title belt.

" don't forget to breathe...very important ! "

The Flame

My pipe

An air chuck and some hose

I had just found and cut

Black tape to hold it all together

This would be my first time smoking weed

Weed

That is what my new guardians called it

When I would sneak and follow them

As they came to this same shed and smoked it themselves

Life was good today

6th Grade

I now lived with some neighbors

The family setting

Everybody agreed

I needed

They had dirt bikes

They had horses

And they had money

As I brought the flame up to stoke my marijuana

I reflected just how I got here

We had snuck out the back

The 2nd door of our current living arrangements

A tin 14x 70, 2×2 framed, green and white trailer

Owned by our youngest sister's father

Me and my little brother

Out to explore the wilderness

By explore

I mean to see just what we could get into

Under the cover of dark

In our trailer park

Being located in the country

In between Norfolk and Madison, Nebraska

Made this even the more adventurous

We were surrounded by fields

Which connected to farms

Which usually contained unlocked barns

These in dire need of our attention

Something about tonight

My stomach feeling a little nauseous

It was that

Or the fact that my mother added a can of cream of mushroom soup

To everything that she cooked

So

Before we set out on our mission

I told my brother that I had to go

Number 2

Take a dump

But

No fear

I had a plan

Previous research had given me all the things

I needed to know

Top of the hill

In the little red Toyota Truck

It will be unlocked

Open the glovebox

A roll of 2 ply

Last trailer on the left

A new addition recently built

A doghouse attached to it

Perfect cover

No electricity

No light

Plus I distinctly remember

A 5-gallon bucket in the shed directly ahead

My utilities assembled

I did the deed

My brother stood guard

Task accomplished

A new dilemma created itself

What to do with the doo-doo?

The evidence

Lucky for us

My brother

In gathering my necessities

Had found a lighter in the glove box of the Toyota

That and a gas can from this shed

We figured should do the trick

We would burn it

Having been the cub scout of the family

I explained to him how this was a particular job

Requiring the special skills which

I had yet to teach him

Therefore

Stand back as

I proceed with the lesson

It was dangerous

I relayed to him

As I would pour out gas from the can

Lighting it with the lighter about mid-flow

The beauty and pure awesomeness of the flames

Lit up the night around us

The look of admiration and excitement

I received from my brother

Each time I would

Just in time

Straighten out the can and stop the flow

Before the flames made their way back up and into the container

Had me brimming with confidence

This and his eagerness eventually won me over

So

I decided to let him give it a try

Under my watchful eye

And following my step by step instructions

Oh

He was a natural

Over and over

I was so proud

Tempting and daring fate

I let him play

As I finished erasing the remaining details of this excursion

It happened so fast

The night was so much brighter

I look over and I see

Fate had struck back

The gas can was completely ablaze

And my little brother was scared

Quickly

I took action

Solution number one

:Take the can from him

Save my brother

Solution number two

Throw the 2-gallon gas can

Now a ball of fire

Standing over 1 foot tall

Into the closet body of water that I could find

The dog dish

The dog dish

Located right in front of the entrance to the doghouse

Which was attached to the addition•

Which had just recently been built

Out of wood

Talk about a flame.

AUTHORS NOTE : The whole place caught fire. Try as we did , running to the pond back and forth for buckets of water...

it did not go well for us !

Escape

1986

I was 14 years old

A detention center

Lincoln, Nebraska

Caught

After running away from my previous facility

Arrested in a stolen vehicle

Here now

Danny

My friend

Accomplice

Standing on top of the pool table

The middle of the facility

Screaming

That's it

We are busting out of here

We have it all planned out

Danny had a pool ball in each hand

Daring any of the staff to come at him

To try and take him down

Now

It was true

Danny

Shelly

Bobby

And I

We had formulated a way out

We had all been arrested together

Determined to leave the same way

But

Danny's pool table stunt

That was nowhere in the plan

The plan

Wait for outside recreation

Jump the fence

Staff surrounded the table

Tackled Danny

Solitary confinement for him

Lock down for the rest of us

One might think

After such a failure

I would give up

Nope

Not me

As a child

I had run away from abuse

I ran away and escaped

It was my only coping mechanism

So

Anytime I was in danger

Or in trouble

I would just run away

So

I made a new plan

I put together a noose in my cell

And I was transferred

Lincoln Regional Center

Psychological Evaluation

Underground tunnels

Connected to the Out Patient Unit

Freedom

Just on the other side

I put on three different sets of clothes

As we headed to the tunnels

It was reccreation time

And the tunnels were the only access

To the gym

We walked

One staff leading

One bringing up the rear

Strategically placed

Toward the back

He would be the only one

That I would have to outrun

I dropped back

I smiled

And I ran with everything I had

I glance back

Nobody

I had lost them

Freedom was just around the corner

Just then

One more long stride

I can't explain it

I did not slip

I did not fall

Somehow I threw my leg

So far out in front of me

It just kept going

Never landing

I slide to the ground in the splits

Something pops

I try to get up

I cannot

I was caught again

Escorted to the hospital

Returning in a wheelchair

I had broken my pelvis

I was sentenced shortly after

The Youth Development Center

Kearney, Nebraska

The day I arrived

Now

Crutches in hand

I had only one thought

Most definitely

Without a doubt...

I am going to escape !

AUTHORS NOTE : The skills we learn , they become our patterns.

And although I continued to try...I NEVER accomplished one success escape !

Prison Life

January 24, 2005

Sentenced to 70 months

The Federal Bureau of Prisons

Medium Security Federal Correctional Institution

Pekin, Illinois

Scared

Not allowed to show it

All the white guys

Housing Unit

Indiana 1

Counting on me

Looking for direction

But only 5 out of the 40

Were out on the tier

Ready to back up my play

My play

None of this

Originally

Had anything to do with me

UFC's Ultimate Fighter

Spike TV

Stephen Bonner and Forest Griffin

Four televisions

One

Always on the sports channel

Keeping the gambling operations live

The other 3

Divided by race

I pretty much stayed away from each

This night was different

This night related closely

To the image that I had managed to create here at the prison

UFC

The Ultimate Fighting Championships

I was the mixed martial artist on the compound

Trained every morning

In my cell

9 a.m.

I was always going to be out of my cell

In the TV Area

On this day

This time

Every week

And it was just on one of these days

That it happened

My cellmate

John

Running down to me

His face flush

Out of breath

He was scared

John explained

He had just been jumped

In our cell

By the Vice Lords

The Vice Lords

A large dominant black gang

They had waited for me to leave

Went in

Pulled him down from the top bunk

Accused of stealing $1000.00 worth

Of hidden tobacco

The beat down

For general purposes

They wanted the cash

Everybody knew

John did not steal

He did not need too

John was the money man

Italian

Ran with the old crew

The problem

John was an easy mark

Rumor was

This had happened before

John had paid

So

When they

Used up all the heroin that they were supposed to sell

John was their solution to their financial issues

I was the wild card

The crazy white boy

That trains every day

Just might be tough

Collectively of course

They knew they would win

But I was enough

To make them wonder

The chances of actual injury to any one of them

I went up to my cell

Took my acoustic guitar

On loan from the music program

Smashed it up against the wall

I pulled a steel rod

Over 12 inches long out of the neck of the guitar

Headed out on the tier

It was NOT Our Cell

It was NOT John's Cell

IT WAS MY CELL

Being my cell

Prison code states

ANYTHING that happens

Gets sold

Goes down in MY CELL

It goes through me first

This code had been violated

If I just let it happen

I would be viewed the same as John

I was not going to let that happen

I was met by 5 members of the gang

Asked if we could chat

I walked into my cell

Steel rod in my hand

Invited them in

Two entered

One sat down

The other stood closer to the doorway

The last 3 remained on the tier

A visual threat to the other inmates

And a look out for the guards

They didn't want me involved

Had nothing to do with me

They meant me no disrespect

I stood my ground

I did not want to have beef with them

I could not win this battle

But

I had to continue to live right here

For the next 2 years

Win lose or draw

I had to take the fight to them

My Cell

My House

And This Is Not Allowed

Or

We could just get started Right Now

I told them

I was aware

I was going to get hurt

But not without hurting some of them

Showing a courage

I did not feel

I asked them to decide which ones were coming in first

They still wanted John

I could not defend

Disprove anything that they were saying

John would have to make his stand

But it was agreed

None of it would happen

In My House

So here I am

The doorman to the mop closet

John and their soldier had entered

It was my job to keep everybody else out

From interfering

As long as I could

It all happened so fast

I dare not turn my head.

As soon as I heard the action start

The brotha standing in front of me

Made a move

Fight or flight

Focused

My left hand gently

Reaches out

Touches his chest

My right hand

The steel rod from the guitar

Time spent sharpening the weapon

A dangerous point

In a voice meant to be

Commanding

Masculine

Instead

Soft as a whisper

I looked him in the eye

One on one brother

One on one

Next thing I know

Soaked with water

The crowd outside the doorway

Dispersing

Guards are running our way

Quickly I spin around

John

Holding their guy on the ground

With one hand

Hitting him with the other

During the struggle

The faucet had been broken off the wall

Water was spraying everywhere

Like the final fight scene

Lethal Weapon.

But

This was not a movie

This just did happen

And

It happened for real

I had survived

For now

I don't exactly know how

Just another normal day

Life in Prison

AUTHORS NOTE : I never had another experience quite like this one, but living in the possibility of it is sometimes even worse !

Outlaw Gunslinger

An associate was accompanying me

Walking out to my car

He to get a torch

I to get the scale and the baggies

Necessities

If we were to accomplish the task at hand

Getting high

And

Dropping of a particular amount of meth

Before moving on to the next stop

BANG

It was loud

In reflection

It was like time slowed down

The echo of the gun shot

Repeated in my ear

Even now

The memory vibrates

Like a strobe light

In my mind

It was loud

Like I heard it

Long before I felt it

I cannot say it was the pain

The pain
Coursing through my right leg

Nor was it the fact
That I had just been standing

Now
Somehow
Finding myself
Face down on the street
In front of my car

No
It wasn't the pain
It was the shock

The shock of the unknown

The process of the events

Registering in my mind

The uncoding of which

Is interrupted

As Iay there watching

The reaction of my companion

Having reached into his truck

To grab a torch

A flame

That we would use

To bring the joy that we seek

Lighting the pipe

Filled with dope

That we had just weighed

The shock

Instead of a torch

He is now holding

An all black

308 Savage Rifle

His eyes scanning the street

The oversized night vision scope

Are you hit ?

Did somebody just shoot you ?

Slowly

My comprehension

Is coming

The throbbing in my leg

Sifting reality back into my mind

Unfolding fact from fiction

This was no Great Western Television Show

No Outlaw Documentary

Jesse James was not here

No

This was only me

Dennis Eugene Cockerham

And I had just shot myself !

AUTHOR'S NOTE : My excuse has always been that the gun was in my waistband at the time. Kicking the car door shut, it went off.

The truth is that I was a felon , high on meth , and carrying a firearm. What could you expect to happen ?

Smokey and The Bandit

A summer night

Bright lights

Police lights

Spot lights

More lights

Than the 4th of July

Police in the street

Police in the yard

You

In the house

Come out with your hands up

In retrospect

Looking back

I now

See clearly

The examples

We set

The lessons learned

By not accepting

Personal responsibility

I had

Created this problem

It was just 3 years ago

I was

Dad

Husband

Friend

Driving

On our way home

It had been

Family night out

Dinner on the town

Stomach full

Parents in the front

Children in the back

The children

Oldest boy 16

Middle girl 12

Baby boy 11

Music

Laughter

Smiles

Happy

Everybody

Just then

It happens

The interruption

The convergence

One life

Splitting into two

Hidden from all

Known to each other

Cellphone rings

On the other end

Panic

Despair

He needed me now

Can I get there

How to explain the moment

That moment

When

In the midst of it all

The addict crosses that line

The unseen

The unplanned

The battle

Fought and lost

In the seconds of indecision

As the wires touch

Cross

In the mind

Sparks fly

The drug wins

Spinning the car around

I was on my way

Blinders on

Focused

All others thoughts

Occupants

Disappeared

There was only me

Me

And

The representation

Of the destination

The urge

The desire

The reciprocation

The idea itself

Firing endorphines

Exploding in my head

The County Sheriff

Chasing him

Him

And the car's supply

Of drugs

Drugs

And the chemicals

Used to make more drugs

Topping the speedometer

2005

4.6 Liter

Ford Mustang

I skid out onto the blacktop

Right behind him

Pedal to the floor

In a burst of acceleration

I passed

Positioning myself

Directly in front of him

A glance back

The rearview mirror

My vision

Seeing

Registering

As if for the first time

Acknowledgement

The backseat

The music

The laughter

The smiles

Gone

The children

Shock

Confusion

Wonder

Fear

What to say

What answers to give

To the questions

Questions

Written on their faces

Seen in their expressions

Engraved in their minds

Smokey and The Bandit kids

Smokey and The Bandit

Now

This summer night

Three years later

Recently released

The hospital

The gunshot wound

The leg

Oldest boy

Out on his own

Middle girl 15

Baby boy 14

Unable to drive

I send them

Return to the hospital

In mom's car

Retrieve my truck

Enroute home

The combustion

Middle girl makes a turn

No blinker

Police

Pulled over

This

All seen

Witnessed

From the windshield

Of my truck

Baby boy behind the wheel

Lights

Camera

Action

Peeling rubber

Tearing up space

Drawing attention

Demanding the chase

Saving his sister

Back

In the garage

I was

As the truck roared

Down the street

Screamed to a halt

In our driveway

Staring in awe

Baby boy runs by me

Fast as he can

Sorry dad

Sorry

Smokey and The Bandit !

AUTHOR'S NOTE : The movie Smokey and The Bandit came out in 1977. Bootlegging beer , the Bandit would drive ahead of the semi transport.

His job was to draw the attention of The Smokey (police) to him and away from the semi. Trust me, it worked way better in the movie !

Use To Live

Call my wife and my son

Tell them that I am sorry

That I love them

All that I had on my mind

That

And of course

The impulse to throw my glass pipe

Full of crystal meth

I wasn't going to make it

This was the end for me

But

If the voice that

I kept hearing in my head

Somehow convinced my body to

HANG ON, HELP WAS COMING

Then I didn't want them to find my pipe

The expansion of thought

Not taking me any further back

Back to the 4.8 grams still in my pocket

Or how I exactly knew that

Having just weighed

Dropped off

7 grams

In a white

Single car garage

Set up as the meeting place

To keep my identity a secret

As if those waiting in the house
Located ten feet away
Would not see
Hear me pull up and enter

Watch me leave
Their anticipation
Of receiving the drugs
For themselves heightened

Back
To having been on this road
Already twice this morning

Or back
To the very instant that I saw him

The decision made to continue forward

Based on a false sense of probability

Calculated by a mind

Which had not had a clear pattern of thought

In over six months

Back

To what exactly happened

What was going on

Sioux Falls, South Dakota

This is where I lived

I was in the wind

Headed east out of town

A blacktop highway

The number of which I cannot remember

In the wind

Mind, and body

Spirit and motorcycle

As one

Brought together

Held that way

By the continuous stream of smoke

That I inhaled

From the end of the glass pipe

Safely secured in my pocket

1st curve

Sway right

Throttle down

Slight seat adjustment

Railroad tracks ahead

2nd curve

Sway right

Throttle up

Stand up

A second set of tracks

All of this for no reason

Just the expansion of motion

To go with the elevated sense

Conjured by my mind

In the midst of my high

Defining the word freedom

Freedom

The sun out and shining

Too early to be too hot

The only breeze is warm

Created by the weight

Me and my machine

Seemingly splitting the atmosphere

Dicing and creating a new reality

Ride to live

Live to ride

Approaching the straight away

Anticipating the habitual thrust of the throttle

The deep rumble of the engine

The tough

The American made

I catch a glimpse

A look again

A verified

Danger resonates somewhere in my senses

Continue with caution

Splitting and dicing

Caution

No

Continue

I continue

In the midst of my addiction

10:30 in the morning

Riding my 1996

Harley Davidson Springer Softail

I hit a deer

I split that deer in half

That deer split me in half

I awoke in the hospital

The only thing on my mind

The 4.8 grams that was in my pocket

I had almost died

My bike had been demolished

Others may have been injured as well

I almost died

The only thought on my mind

The drugs

My singular purpose

My obsession

My Life

I had lived to use

Used to live

This time

This time I had used

To almost die

AUTHOR'S NOTE : I did not stop using even after this. It was the deer's fault not the drugs.

An addict loses his home...housing problem

An addict loses his job...employment problem

An addict loses his wife...relationship problem

An addict sells the family car for dope...transportation problem

NEVER *does the addict say...it is a drug problem !*

A New High

The last thing

That I remember

About being high

I was underneath a car

For 7 days straight

Trying to change a muffler

I didn't even have one tool !

But not this day

This day

There were 24 go karts

Only 8 allowed on the track

At any given time

24 addicts

Behind the wheel of each

Engines running

I had been arrested again

Released to a halfway house

Pre-trial

One of the requirements

Attend two 12 Step Meeting a week

Putting this in proper perspective

I had been through all of this before

Many treatments

Many times

I knew that I did not want to do meth

I also knew

As did my family

That I would not be around

When the sentencing date came

My goal was simple

Stay out long enough

To help my family get stable

That

And organize my plan

To escape law enforcement

In order to do that

I figured

I should remain clean

Attending these meetings

I started to like a few people

I even shared sometimes

I was honest

About why I was there

Honest about not believing

Any of this

Could ever help me

A picnic

Pie in the face

Go karts

A local track

Up the road from my apartment

Sounded like a good time

This was an activity

Scheduled for members

I decided to attend

When the flag rose

We all floored it

All carts were on the track

It seemed

At the same time

Is some even going

Is the wrong direction

All

Involved in a private game

Crash up Derby

I can still hear

The track handler's anxiety

As he got on his walkie talkie

Radioed for backup

I know that we retired

At least

5 of those karts that day

I am still amazed

At the thought

We didn't get kicked out

It was havoc

It was crazy

Most of all

It was fun

That day

At the track

It changed my outlook

If these people

Could do this for me

Bring me

This much fun

Well then

I was willing to chase that

With the same intensity

That I had chased the dope !

AUTHOR'S NOTE : It is easy to tell an addict to stop using, Harder for them to do. I believed , at that time , that I used for fun.

That day, that reason was taken away.

Hideaway

Mr. Recovery

That was me

I was completely sold on the 12 steps

This whole new way of life

I was working a program

I had just received

My 6th month clean time coin

The judge had seen fit

To allow me

To be released home

From the halfway house

M-C-K-A-Y-L-A !!!

My wife yelled

She was in a complete panic

If this was an emergency

She needed our daughter's help

And she needed it now

It is said

The disease of addiction

Cunning and baffling

That an addict

Even a clean one

Could convince themselves

Of some pretty different things

I had just received a letter

In the mail

From the federal court system

Right away

I assumed

This letter was an accident

I knew that they would be coming

To arrest me

Any minute

But

This time

I had the advantage

I knew that they were coming

I must think quickly

They would catch on soon

Be coming any time

I hollered at my wife

Come to the living room

I proceeded

Taking the cushions off our couch

Then

I pulled out the hide-a-bed

Grabbing the mattress

Taking it off the bed

I lay down on the frame

My dutiful wife

Looking at me like I was crazy

Did not hesitate one second

As I instructed her

To fold me up into that couch

Being off drugs

I had gained some weight

Halfway up
She had lost control

Like a pig in a blanket
My body surrounded
By the metal frame

I just fell right into
The inside makings
Of what was our couch

My daughter
Answering the call of her mother
Running from her room
The back of the apartment

You can imagine

Her expression

I was stuck in the couch

And what must have looked

Like a beached whale

Taking a water plunge

Gone bad

My wife had tried and tried

Lift

Pull

Flip

She could not get me out

An addict

My best thinking

Literally

Got me right here

Now

In the midst of the chaos

That I definitely

Created for myself

That same thinking is telling me

This just might work !

AUTHOR'S NOTE : It is hard to desribe the patterns of thought that are inherited by the addict.

To come to the understanding that one cannot rely on their own thinking. This is the most difficult thing to overcome.

Drug use does not just change my perception of reality. The reality is that it changes the way my brain works to perceive it all together.

Whether I was high or not !

Recovery On The Run

Cuba

No extradition

Sitting in a dance club
I almost had paid off

It was connected
By an inside door
To the gentleman's club
I had just built

This all in memory
Of another place
One that my mother had managed

Back in the 90's

Yankton, South Dakota

I had heard it said

God gave us memories

So that we could have roses

In December

This was my way

Of watering those roses

I was still on the wagon

Living Clean and Serene

Matter of fact

I brought the 12 Steps

To Cuba

Created a Home Group

It was called R.I.P.

Recovery In Person

And that is what it said

On the front of each t-shirt

That I made and sold

For the group's 7th Tradition

On the back

A simple

But graphic design

A tombstone

In a graveyard

Reading

R.I.P. to drugs, alcohol,

And all other addictions

Since the desire to use

Had been lifted from me

I was able to hang out
Here
In these bars
What better way for me
To share the message
Find the addict
That still suffers

Plus
I needed these places

Needed them to clean my money
To make me a local
A part of the economy

My money
Just how it had taken me this far

So many bottles of Purple Degreaser

Bought from The Family Dollar

The one dollar bills

Soaked

Then heated in a bowl filled with it

3 minutes per bowl

10 bills each

The buzzer goes off

Take them out

Wipe them clean

No more ink

Drying them on the counter

Taping them together

Blue painter's tape

All the way across the states

To the Florida Keys

Legally

U.S. Citizens at this time

Could not enter Cuba

The fastest alternative

Mexico

Through California or Texas

Then

A flight from there

Passports

Visas

Possible identification needed

I decided against it

AUTHOR'S NOTE : It is woth noting here. I used drugs to escape reality as it was..

I brought this pattern of thought into my recovery without even being aware of it. This is documentation of this realizartion.

Once I knew that I was the author of my own story, then it was my choice to write fact or fiction.

Tomatoes and Corn

I was scared

So scared

There was going to be a fight

It was going to be my fault

The kids

They should not

Have to go through this

I wish

They didn't have to see it

The rush of memories

Previous battles

The children

Uncertain

Stability

Like a house built on sand

Never knowing

Just when

The foundation was going to shift

The basic necessities

Afforded to every child

From their parents

Food

Water

Shelter

Love

Security

These All

Stripped from them before

In the blink of an eye

What they thought was reality

What they knew

As their lives

Their family

Completely flipped

Gone

Like the electricity

Shut off

For a second time

A padlock now on the box

A warning

Illegally

It had been turned back on

Gone

Like the food

In the cabinets

In the frig

Gone

Mandatory attended suppers

To go over everybody's day

The favorite brunch

Pancakes

Bacon

Eggs

Heated syrup on the weekend

And eventually

Gone

There very house

Thought to be home

Locked changed

Access forbidden

Their teenage identities

Their

Possessions

Still inside

I was scared

They had no idea

This was coming

I had decided to go for it

Recovery

I had taken

The whole idea of running

Off the table

I had a Sponsor

I was working the steps

Taking a moral inventory

Acknowledging

The wreckage of my past

My part in things

The span of time that covered

All that I had done

What I had become

Who I really was

Who I really was

I didn't know anymore

With each step that I took
What I defined as me
Was disassembled before my eyes

Like a picture in reverse

Becoming a puzzle
Then just a million little pieces
Found in a box
Now called my life

I was headed home after a meeting
A talk with my sponsor

I told him
I didn't know
Something was happening to me

I was confused

I didn't even know
If I wanted to be
With my wife anymore

I love her
Not looking for anybody else
Not wanting to leave
Or move out

Not wanting to cause her
Or the family
Anymore pain either

I just didn't know what to do

Sharing these feelings
It was new to me

Being told

I needed to share them

With the one

I was feeling them about

Almost took me over the edge

No good could come of that

I argued

I presented the facts of my case

Built from stats of the past

Physical violence

Police

Jail

Not happening !

My reality

No longer based on deceit

He instructed me

Deceit breeds deceit

Deceit was the destruction

Not the foundation

Of my relationship

My recovery

If I wanted the same results

That I had always got

Then I could do

What I had always done

If I wanted something different

I could try his suggestion

Do something different

Be honest

You can't eat tomatoes
And shit corn

It just cannot be done

Physically shaking
Fear
Coming from a depth
I could not comprehend

Going against
Everything that I knew

Knew
Without a doubt

Dry heaves

Coughing

Choking

It is me against me

I am scared

In our kitchen

Our newly formed home

Two bedroom apartment

Shared

Son daughter and grandfather

I tell her

When I am done

She asks me to stand

She walks over to me

She puts her arms around me

She gives me

The most affectionate hug

I have ever felt

She looked me in the eye

Told me that she loved me

She knew I loved her

That it was okay

She would be right here

Until I figured it out

WHO KNEW

You cannot eat tomatoes

And shit corn

It just cannot be done !

AUTHOR'S NOTE : *To ask yourself if everything that you are doing, saying, or how you understand things...*

Is it working for you ? Are you getting the results that you want ?

If not, you might have to try something different. That something different usually has to come from somebody different.

Somebody other then yourself.

From Me To You

The United States

Federal Bureau Of Prisons

Home to the most

Notorious Outlaws

Prisoners

Never expected to be free again

That

Or those with so many years

The mental anguish

The possibility of freedom

They would be better off without it

That is where I found myself

Inmate # 05320-030

There but not there

I was

As I wrote this

Located in Yankton

South Dakota

Federal Prison Camp

One easily mistaken

As a beautiful park

In the center of town

Once a college

There were no fences

No razor wire

No killers

Sentenced to 55 months

The judge recognized

My rehabilitation

Allowed me

To self-surrender

Sentenced me

To show up

To a predesignated prison

On a specific day

To start serving time

On my own free will !

A lot has changed

Recovery

While on the streets

I achieved 18 months clean

Knowing

I was coming to prison

Choosing

Learning

Living

Surrendering

I was happy to find myself here

Able to continue this journey

I completed an intensive treatment

Offered at the camp

I continued to be an active member

In the 12 Step Program

I accredited

To giving me my life back

I enrolled

In a Creative Writing Program

Taught by a professor

From the local University

Inspired

To share my story

My message

To learn how to express it

In the words I wrote down

This has been that story

My message of hope

My promise of freedom

Fragmented

Scattered

Yet complete at the same time

A lot like my life

I am an Addict

My name is Dennis

Notes

August 23, 2021

I am home now

Sioux Falls

South Dakota

Released

On my wife's birthday

Home Confinement

Ankle Monitor for GPS

Until Febuary

Life is new

Life is great

I have a new perspective
I have a new plan

Mowing the lawn
First time in years

A hill in our front yard
Quite the work out

Only two rows to go
The wife joins me outside

Having seen my persistence
My struggle
Focused as I am
Complete the task at hand

Defeating this hill of grass

She politely stops me

Informs me

If I would just pull in

The lever

Located right on the bar

I was using to push the mower

Those front wheels

Would go

All by themselves

The mower was self-propelled

Ha !

I guess I still have a lot to learn !